# Dear Pare~

Buckle up! You are about to join y~
exciting journey. The destinatic

Road to Reading will help you ~ ~ere. The program
offers books at five levels, or Mile~ ~pany children from their
first attempts at reading to successfu~ ~ng on their own. Each
Mile is paved with engaging stories anu uelightful artwork.

### Getting Started
For children who know the alphabet and are eager
to begin reading
• easy words  • fun rhythms  • big type  • picture clues

### Reading With Help
For children who recognize some words and sound out
others with help
• short sentences  • pattern stories  • simple plotlines

### Reading On Your Own
For children who are ready to read easy stories by themselves
• longer sentences  • more complex plotlines  • easy dialogue

### First Chapter Books
For children who want to take the plunge into chapter books
• bite-size chapters  • short paragraphs  • full-color art

### Chapter Books
For children who are comfortable reading independently
• longer chapters  • occasional black-and-white illustrations

There's no need to hurry through the Miles. Road to Reading is
designed without age or grade levels. Children can progress at their
own speed, developing confidence and pride in their reading ability no
matter what their age or grade.

**So sit back and enjoy the ride—every Mile of the way!**

*Library of Congress Cataloging-in-Publication Data*
Coxe, Molly.
Fox trot / written and illustrated by Molly Coxe.
     p.   cm. — (Road to reading. Mile 2)
Summary: Fox gets a band and the other animals all dance to the music.
ISBN 0-307-26209-X (pbk.)
[1. Bands (Music)—Fiction.  2. Dancing—Fiction.  3. Foxes—Fiction.
4. Animals—Fiction.  5. Stories in rhyme.]  I. Title.  II. Series.
PZ8.3.C8395Fo   1999
[E]—dc21                                                        98-38485
                                                                CIP
                                                                AC

**A GOLDEN BOOK • New York**
Golden Books Publishing Company, Inc. New York, New York  10106

ISBN: 0-307-26209-X                                    A MCMXCIX

# FOX TROT

## by Molly Coxe

# Fox has a plan.

Fox gets a band.

"What's that?" says Pig.

"What's that?" says Frog.

# "What's that?" says Cat.

"It's a band!" says Fox.

12

Fox does the fox trot.

Pig does the jig.

# Frog does the hip-hop.

# Cat does the cha-cha-cha.

Fox has a plan.

Fox gets a pan.

"What's that?" says Pig.

"What's that?" says Frog.

"What's that?" says Cat.

"It's a pan!" says Fox.

Fox does the fox trot.

Pig does the jig.

Frog does the hip-hop.

Cat does the
cha-cha-cha.

# Fox has a plan.

# Fox forgets the band.

"What's that?" says Pig.

"What's that?" says Frog.

"What's that?" says Cat.

"It's the band!" says Fox.

28

Fox does the fox trot.

Pig does the jig.

Frog does the hip-hop.

Cat does the cha-cha-cha.